HUNGARY

For all the children in the world; may you forever stay
curious about the world around you - K.J.

Dedicated to my Hungarian husband and to all our Hungarian ancestors. - K.J.

Published by Sloth Dreams Publishing LLC
Pennsylvania, USA

http://www.SlothDreams.com/kids

My Country
HUNGARY
Written & Illustrated by
KeriAnne Jelinek
www.SlothDreams.com
All Rights Reserved under International and
Pan-American Copyright Conventions.
Published in the United States by Sloth Dreams
Publishing. Originally published in 2022.

Hungary is on the continent of Europe. Europe is not a country. Europe is a continent.

A continent is a large mass of land that has many different countries within it. Each country is entirely unique and different from any other country. Each and every country has its own food, language, culture, music and traditions.

SLOVAKIA
Kraków
Košice
Bratislava
RAINE
Budapest
HUNGARY
Szeged
RO
Timiș
Zagreb
TIA
Sava
Bel
Istanbul
DENMARK
GERMAN
BELARUS
Barcelona

Hungary is a country that is about the size of Indiana in the United States.

Hungary is a country found in Central Europe. It is a landlocked country with many borders.

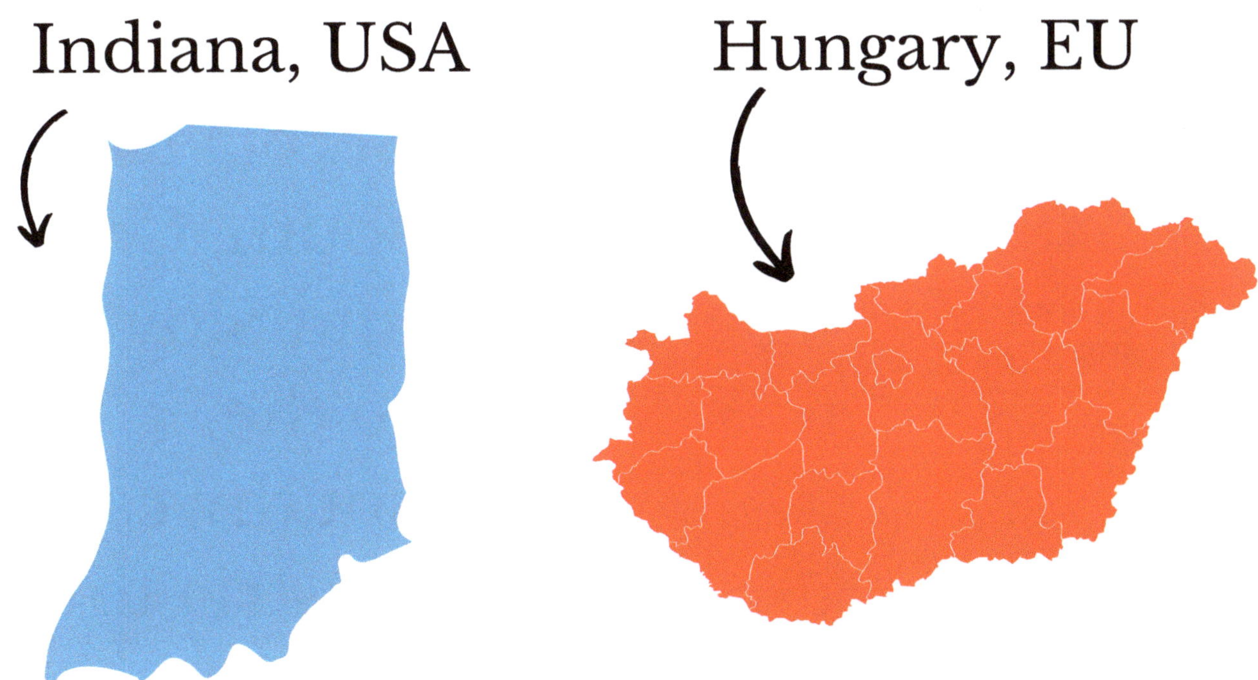

Hungary shares borders with Slovakia to the north, Ukraine to the northeast, Romania to the east, Serbia to the south, Croatia and Slovenia to the southwest, and Austria to the west.

The Capital of Hungary is Budapest. It is the largest city in Hungary. Other major cities are Debrecen, Szeged, and Miskolc.

The National Flag is a tri-colour flag with red, green, and white. It has been the official flag of Hungary since 1957.

The combination of colors is a symbol for Hungarian history originating from the 18th and 19th centuries. Today, the flag stands for the national freedom movement and for Hungarian independence.

The two main religions of Hungary are
Catholic and Non-religious or Agnostic.
The catholic religion has many saints and
martyrs. Saint Martin of Tours is the most
famous religious figure in Hungary. St.
Kinga of Poland is also a very famous saint
in the catholic church of Hungary.

Hungarians celebrate many holidays. Some of the most popular holidays are: St. Sylvester (New Year's Day), Day of Hungarian Revolution (March 15), Easter, St. Istvan's Day (August 20), Republic Day (October 23), All Saint's Day (November 1) and Christmas.

Christmas is celebrated on Christmas Eve (December 24). Often Christmas trees are decorated with gingerbread cookies (*mézeskalács*) shaped into classic Christmas shapes, such as bells, angels, and stars.

Delicious *bejgli,* a sweet yeast bread with poppy seeds or walnut filling is often laid out on the table for a Christmas treat.

Hungary has many Easter traditions. Painting Easter eggs is a very common tradition. Geometric designs, and ornamental swirls are popular designs for Hungarian Easter eggs. They often use various paints, dyes, brushes and sometimes books of patterns for inspiration. Some artisans make beautiful eggs that have stunning patterns that require special tools, wax and dipping methods.

The most famous food that comes from Hungary is goulash (*gulyas*). Goulash is a delicious stew that has chunks of beef, vegetables and the world famous, Hungarian paprika. Some other common Hungarian foods include: *lángos*, a deep-fried bread topped with cheese and sour cream, *paprikás csirke* (Paprika Chicken), *dobostorta* (a chocolate sponge cake layered with a delicious buttercream frosting, and topped with a layer of thick caramel), *rétes* (a strudel like pastry filled with sweet fruit paste, such as cherries or apples), *meggyleves* (a sweet cherry soup made of cream, sugar and cherries), and Hungarian Stuffed Bell Peppers.

MEGGYES MÁKOS
POPPYSEED
MÁKOS

Hungary has many crops and farmland. The top farms produce wheat, corn, sunflower seeds and rapeseed oils. Paprika (Bell Peppers) are also grown widely. Grapes and famous wines are large exports for Hungary. Some other specialty foods that Hungary is well known for are: salami, poultry, pork, special sausages and goose liver.

Paprika, the Hungarian word for bell pepper, is a large part of Hungarian culture. Paprika's give a very distinct flavor to almost all Hungarian cuisine. The spice flavors most of the stews, soups and dishes, such as, chicken paprika and goulash. The bell pepper has become somewhat of a symbol or icon for the Hungarian culture to people around the world.

PRIDE OF
SZEGED
HUNGARIAN
PAPRIKA
BUDAPEST
HUNGARY

Hungarian paprika's (bell peppers), come in many different colors. They can be yellow, red, orange, green and even purple. Bell peppers come in many different flavors from sweet and mild to spicy and bold.

Bell peppers are dried and ground into the spice, paprika. There are eight grades of Hungarian paprikas ranging from sweet and mild to pungent, more pungent, noble and sweet, and semi-sweet.

Paprika from Hungary is a highly prized product that is one of the best paprika's in the world. Paprika has been a very important part of Hungarian culture throughout history and is still a very important part of Hungary's identity as a country today.

Weather in Hungary can vary throughout the year. In summer it is hot with low humidity. Winters can be frigid, cold, snowy and rainy. The average annual temperature is around 49 degrees Fahrenheit with it ranging between 26-81 degrees Fahrenheit seasonally.

The people of Hungary speak Hungarian. The Hungarian or *Magyar* language is part of the Finno-Ugric group in the Uralic language family. *Magyar* has many accented letters and letter sounds made up of two letters combined. There are forty-four Hungarian symbols in the Hungarian alphabet.

Macska - **Cat**

Dob - **Drum**

Pillango - **Butterfly**

Hungary's official money is the *forint* (HUF). The *forint* has been the money of Hungary since August 1946.

The traditional clothing of Hungary consists of the beautiful embroidered shirts called the *kalocsai*. Women and girls also wear a traditional flowered or embroidered dress called the *matyó*. It is traditional for women to wear pearl necklaces with their traditional clothing

Traditional Hungarian clothing consist of the *kalocsai* (embroidered shirt), a dress for girls called the *matyó*. Under the skirts, they may wear a linen underskirt called the *pendely*. Hungarian women often wear from 4-10 baggy skirts over the *pendely* to accentuate the size and shape of the outer skirt and the hip.

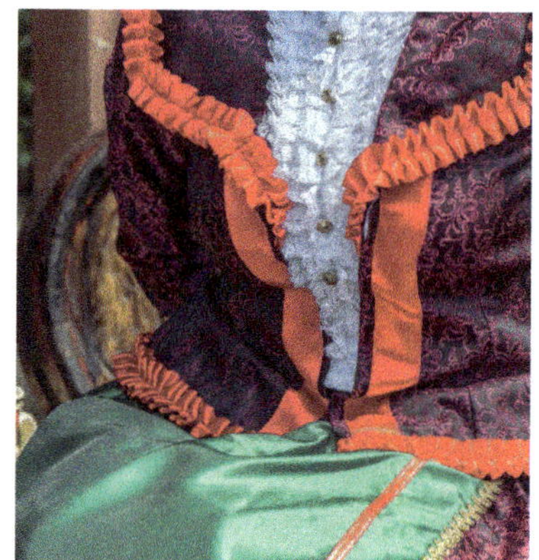

Both men and women often wear an apron or a belt around their waists. Women and girls were ribbons around their waists, shoulders, and in their hair. Men and women often wear a sheepskin shawl around their chest and shoulders called an *elejbor*. Sheepskin and animal furs are often worn to keep warm and are also decorative to their clothing.

Traditional clothing for men and boys are: vests *(jerkins)* over linen shirts, fur coats, animal furs and special linen underpants. Men wear hats, caps and coifs. Often, hats are decorated with feathers or other hat ornaments, such as pins.

Women wear special head scarves, flower wreaths, ribbons or decorative hats.

The people of Hungary typically have light golden or olive colored skin tones. They have a variety of hair and eye colors. Pale blue, blue, green or brown eyes and blonde, brown or black hair are typical features of Hungarians. The genetic makeup of Hungarians is very diverse.

Over thousands of years, many wars, conquests and realms, Hungary has had genetic influences from around the world. Long ago the Turkish Ottoman Empire, Austro-Germanic ethnic groups, Finnish groups, Turkish and Slavic ethnic groups ruled Hungary. In addition, there are some minority ethnic groups that also have genetic influence upon Hungarians. The largest of these groups are the *Romani* or *Gypsies*.

The Hungarian *Romani*, often called *gypsies*, are the largest minority group in Hungary. The Romani people are one of the last wandering nomadic people in all of Europe. Often, this minority group, has been segregated and ostracized from all aspects of Hungarian life.

The Romani people have a very unique culture and have very distinct physical characteristics. Hungarian gypsies also have a very rich musical tradition that is known throughout the world. There are many, many famous musicians that come from the Romani lineage. Many famous composers, violinists, singers and pianist come from the Hungarian Romani ancestral heritage.

Today, it is believed that all Hungarians are a mix of Finno-Ugric Magyars, Turkic, Slavic and Germanic ethnicities.

Hungary has a long history of many cultural influences upon their country. Turkey, Finland, several Slavic countries, Austria and Germany all have contributed to the genetic makeup of the Hungarian people. The physical features vary widely within the country.

Special landmarks are not only tourist attractions, but special monuments to the Hungarian people's past ancestors and ancestral heritage.

Szechenyi Thermal Baths, Budapest

Fisherman's Bastion, Budapest

Some of the famous landmarks include: the Hungarian Parliament Building, Szechenyi Thermal Baths, Buda Castle, Fisherman's Bastion, Szechenyi Bridge, Memento Park, and St. Stephen's Basilica. Lake Balaton is a freshwater lake that is very popular. It is surrounded by beaches, volcanic hills and has many fancy hotels along the shoreline.

Szechenyi Bridge

St. Stephen's Basilica

Memento Park

Lake Balaton

Buda Castle

Hungarian Parliament Building

The Hungarian Parliament building is a destination you don't want to miss. It sits on the eastern bank of the Danube River and is a classic example of Neo-Gothic architecture. It has influences of Gothic, Baroque, and Renaissance architecture throughout. It is the third largest parliament building in the world. It boasts 691 interior rooms, 12.5 miles of staircases, 10 courtyards, and 88 statues of Hungarian rulers. King Steven's crown jewels are on display, as are many rooms filled with art from throughout the centuries.

Lake Balaton is a very popular destination for vacations and holiday celebrations. The hilly north shore is home to very famous wine-growing vineyards. The region has protected wetlands and beautiful scenic hiking trails at the Balaton Uplands National Park.

Hungary is well known for its geo-thermal baths. Szechenyi Thermal Baths is the grand champion of thermal spas. People from all around the world flock to these baths for their healing properties and health benefits. These thermal waters are said to heal many kinds of skin ailments, such as acne and eczema. The mineral content of the water is also said to help heal internal diseases. Bathing helps circulation in the body, cell oxygenation, and detoxification of cells. The heat of the water also is beneficial for pain management, as it helps to alleviate sensations of pain.

The tulip is
Hungary's
national
flower.

The national symbol
and animal of
Hungary is the *Turul*,
a mythological
falcon-eagle-like
bird. It originated
with the Turkic
people. It has
become the national
symbol of Hungary.

The Hungarian coat of arms has the Holy Crown of Hungary of Saint Stephen on the top. The white stripes symbolize the "four silver rivers". The double cross represents the northern ranges or lands of Hungary. The symbols date back to the Middle Ages.

The national dog of Hungary is the Hungarian *Vizsla*. They have a short sleek coat that is brown or reddish in color. They are adapted well for hunting and sport.

Kuvasz

Puli

Komondor

Viszla's are very popular dogs in the United States and in other countries worldwide. Other dog's from Hungary include the: *Komondor*, *Kuvasz* and the *Puli*.

Viszla

Hungarian dance is very popular with children, teens and adults alike. Most dancing is traditional folk dance.

The most popular kind of dance is the *czardas* (a spirited dance with energetic movements and rhythms). The *ugrós* (jumping dance) and the *karikázó* (circle dance) performed by women and accompanied by singing folksongs), are other popular dances.

The most common instruments in Hungarian music are the: cimbalom, hurdy-gurdy, bagpipe, violin, tambourine, various woodwind instruments and the *ütőgardon*.

Bagpipe

Hurdy-Gurdy

Cimbalom

Violin

ütőgardon

Hungary has many musical traditions. Some of those traditions are Hungarian folk songs and folk music. Folk music is highly distinctive, having difficult rhythms and complex melodies based on the pentatonic scale and major seconds and minor thirds.

Folk music is based heavily upon text and vocals. Vocal music is a very important to traditional folk music of Hungary.

There are some very famous musicians that come from Hungary. Ferenc "Franz" Liszt is by far the most famous pianist, conductor and composer that comes from Hungary. He is considered one of the greatest pianists to have ever lived. Béla Bartók is also an extremely famous composer of Hungarian music. Zoltán Kodály is famous for his Kodály Method of teaching music. Some other famous musicians are: George Szell (Conductor), Miklós Rózsa (Academy Award winning film score composer), Livia Zita (Singer and voiceover actress), Peter Bence (Pianist of Despacito), and world famous György Fischer (Pianist).

Franz (*Ferenc*) Liszt

There are many, many famous musicians that come from Hungary. Many pianists, composers, conductors and musicians come from Hungary. There is a long, rich cultural heritage of classical music and musicians that come from Hungary.

From classical, traditional music to folk music and other popular genres of music, Hungarians have musicians and music of every style.

Béla Bartók

Zoltán Kodály

Joseph Pulitzer was originally a newspaper publisher who became a politician crusading against corruption. He founded the Columbia school of journalism. The Pulitzer Prize, a world-renowned award, annually rewards excellence in various fields, is named in his honor.

Many famous people come from Hungary. Erno Rubik, a professor and sculptor, invented the Rubik's Cube, one of the most popular games in the world.

Harry Houdini, a famous magician, escape artist and daredevil was born in Budapest, Hungary and lived much of his life in Hungary.

EUROPE'S ECLIPSING SENSATION
HOUDINI
THE WORLD'S HANDCUFF KING & PRISON BREAKER
NOTHING ON EARTH
CAN HOLD
HOUDINI
A PRISONER

Hungarian arts and crafts are very popular pastimes. Traditional crafts, including: embroidery, lace making, furniture making and pottery are all common hobbies. Musical instrument making is also a beloved pastime.

This beautiful embroidery is revered as a symbol for Hungary. It is referred to as the *Tulip Motif.* It stands for divinity and femininity. It is a very popular design for dishware, linens, doilies and other decorative household items, including clothing.

Csikos, or Hungarian cowboys, are a true cultural icon. These *csikos* have been riding the range near Hortobagy National Park on the Great Hungarian Plains (*Puszta*) for thousands of years. *Csikos* ride horseback while criss-crossing the plains in bright blue loose-fitting pants, shirts, black vests, black boots and wide brimmed hats. These *Magyar csikos* also have ranches and put on shows of equestrian showmanship for tourist.

The country of Hungary is overflowing with beautiful customs and incredible people. The people of Hungary have endured many hardships over thousands of years. They have had many wars and many kingdoms that have taken over their land. Hungarians are a strong and resilient people that don't stand down in the face of hardships. They are hospitable, traditional, kind, loyal and they love a good meal. Their customs and traditions are sacred to the lovable people of Hungary.